Secrets to Success

32 Entrepreneurs Reveal the Best Advice they have Ever Received

Paul B. Thornton

First Edition

Multi-Media
P u b l i c a t i o n s Inc.
Oshawa, Ontario, Canada

**Secrets to Success: 32 Entrepreneurs Reveal
the Best Advice they have Ever Recieved**
by Paul B. Thornton

Managing Editor:	Kevin Aguanno
Copy Editor:	Peggy LeTrent
Typesetting:	Peggy LeTrent
Cover Design:	Troy O'Brien

Published by:
Multi-Media Publications Inc.
Box 58043, Rosslynn RPO
Oshawa, ON, Canada, L1J 8L6

http://www.mmpubs.com/

Paperback   ISBN-10: 1554890586 ISBN-13: 9781554890583
Adobe PDF ebook ISBN-10: 1554890594 ISBN-13: 9781554890590

Published in Canada.

CIP data available from the publisher.

Table of Contents

Introduction

The March 21, 2005 issue of *Fortune* magazine included an article titled "The Best Advice I ever Got." It was a great article that offered wit and wisdom from top business leaders. It motivated us to produce this e-book. The following compilation focuses on the "best advice" people received in helping them start and run a successful business.

Entrepreneurs

Don Katz, Wine Director

WWW.SYMPOSIUMWINEBAR.COM

The best advice my parents ever gave me was go to college. Considering that I wanted to drop out every semester of my degree program in Hospitality Management this was not easy advice to follow. Now that I own my own business I think they are quite proud. My first lesson from a professor was to use someone else's money to open a business. My dad is still thanking the professor for that one! Another professor taught me to survey all my skills and market myself. Since going blind, I recognized my newly enhanced sense of taste and smell are my new best assets. I used these refined skills to market myself and open Symposium Wine Bar where the focus is on pouring blind friendly wines.

Thomas A. Goodrow

FOUNDER AND CHAIR EMERITUS OF THE NACCE (NATIONAL
ASSOCIATION COMMUNITY COLLEGE ENTREPRENEURSHIP)
BOARD OF DIRECTORS

Focus, Focus, Focus! This by far is the best advice I have learned through personal experience. Do one thing better than everyone else, no matter what it is, and you'll enjoy entrepreneurial success. Fight off all temptations to be distracted and unfocused by entertaining opportunities that compete with your core entrepreneurial mission, otherwise you'll become vulnerable to your competition. Lastly, take time to listen to everyone but always remember to follow no one, except your peaceful balance of intuition and intellect.

Adam Boyce

FOUNDER AND PRESIDENT DREAM ESSENTIALS

Many years ago I read a famous book "Think and Grow Rich" by Napolean Hill. The author had interviewed many of the most influential people to determine what made them successful. The conclusion—successful people are goal-setters. I set goals on a regular basis. I've found if I know what I want, then the means to achieve my goal will appear. Starting a successfully business is something that doesn't just happen immediately, it comes slowly in stages. I knew my ultimate goal and the stairway to my dreams have miraculously appeared for me to climb.

Ed Zimmer

FOUNDER AND PRESIDENT
ZIMMER FOUNDATION (TENONLINE.ORG)

The best advice I ever received (from an uncle in my pre-teens) was "build your vocabulary". I'm sure his intent was that I learn to communicate clearly and precisely. However, I later learned that advice was the secret to gaining a quick understanding of any new field, technology, or discipline. Once you've learned its special vocabulary, you have a grasp on all of its key concepts—and as an added benefit, find yourself accepted as a "peer".

The best advice I can give (based on 60 years of entrepreneuring in many different businesses) is "focus on your customers."

Jennifer Gonzales
CEO, PROCHARMS, INC.

The best business advice I ever got was from Craig McCaw back in the early 1990's when he owned Cellular One. He paid a personal visit to our office in Sacramento, CA, making an inspiring presentation that impacted me greatly. His self-described business philosophy was "keep it simple", a basic idea that has been a valuable asset to me not only in business but also in everyday life. I relied heavily on that principle as we grew our business from the ground up. I think it is much more than just a philosophy...it is a way of life, and has become a big part of who I am today. Whenever something begins to spiral out of control, I go back to the beginning and remind myself to "keep it simple". It works every time!

About Jennifer Gonzales'

When Jennifer Gonzales' husband, John, gave her an Italian charm bracelet for Valentine's Day in 2002, Jennifer - a huge

Sacramento Kings fan - searched in vain for a Kings charm before deciding to create one herself.

She visited the Team Store at Arco Arena to ask about licensing, and a helpful employee called Kings' co-owner Gavin Maloof and let Jennifer leave a message. She was stunned when Maloof returned her call and directed her to a contact at Arco.

Jennifer recruited her first rep - a charm-store business owner—and they collected a 20% deposit from interested charm retailers across the country. Jennifer and John set up a work space in their living room for the charms. "Everyone who knew us thought we were crazy", says Jennifer.

After four months, they moved into a small office and began hiring employees. The company's growth has allowed them to expand from the original charm line into a full line of Pro and Collegiate jewelry and accessories. Jennifer and John were featured in the summer issue of *Entrepreneurs Be Your Own Boss* that featured young entrepreneurs who started multi-million dollar businesses in their home.

Nadja Piatka
FOUNDER AND PRESIDENT, NADJA FOODS

I've been fortunate to have received valuable advice in my personal life that has helped me achieve success in business. A friend and mentor taught me to be open, have passion and purpose, and be willing to share my struggles.

I went through a difficult period before I started my business. After being a stay-at-home mom for twenty years, I found myself an unemployable single parent after my husband left. I didn't want people to know that I was being pursued by creditors. I was ashamed and embarrassed. The lowest point occurred when I forced my young daughter to hide with me under the table. A bill collector was peering in the windows and I didn't want him to see us. Several years later when my business became a success I was chosen to receive a very special award called "Woman of Vision" by a local TV station. My daughter came home from college to attend the awards luncheon. In my speech I wanted to show her that regardless of what we went through, success and pride was attainable through hard work.

I was ashamed to tell our secret, but my mentor said that it was my purpose to share the story and help others who had been through difficult times. I didn't know how the audience would respond. I stood at the podium, looked straight at my daughter and said "Veronica, today we are sitting at the table instead of under it". The audience burst into applause and many told me that it brought tears to their eyes and gave them hope to achieve their own dreams. I continue to share my story in the hope of helping others through their difficult times.

About Nadja Piatka

Nadja Piatka is the founder and President of Nadja Foods, the Ultimate Girls Getaway and the author of 2 Best Selling Books.

As an unemployable single mother of two, plagued by creditors and no income, she began baking muffins and brownies at home and testing them on her two teenage children. She was soon selling her baked goods to local coffee shops. When her customer base grew, she commissioned a local bakery to "out source" and deliver her products.

With a one hundred dollar investment she grew her business from her kitchen to becoming a international supplier to the food industry. Nadja has appeared on many TV shows including the Oprah Winfrey Show and The Big Idea with Donny Deutsch.

Today Nadja Foods supplies her great tasting Healthy Brownies, Petite Angel Cakes and new Organic Cookies to customers across the United States and Canada. Nadja donates 5% of her profits from the sale of her online Organic Cookies to the American Heart Association and Feeding America.

Nadja tours as a motivational speaker sharing her amazing professional and personal story of building her business, surviving leukemia, being an unemployed single parent and cherishing every moment in life.

Nadja has written two best selling cookbooks, the first was, *The Joy of Losing Weight*.

Nadja is a Recipe Developer, Volunteer and Spokesperson for the American Heart Association and sits on their Board of Directors for the Northeast Region.

She was inducted into the Twenty First Century Business Women's Hall of Fame, Bay Path College, MA. She sits on the Niagara University Business Administration Advisory Board. She is also a former food columnist where she specialized in recipe "Makeovers" to promote healthy eating.

Nadja was the recipient of the Regional Award for the Canadian Woman Entrepreneur of the Year and recognized as one of the ITV News WOMEN OF VISION.

As a member of the Small and Medium Enterprise Task Force, an Advisory Board for the Department of Foreign Affairs and International Trade, Nadja contributed to developing a report on "Canadian Business and Exporting."

Paul J. Kozub
Creator and founder of V-One Vodka.

The best advice I ever received was not spoken, it was from watching and listening. My father started his own craft business from nothing and grew it into a multi-million dollar company. I don't think there was any secrete to his success, it was pure sweat and determination. He worked 18 hour days and made a number of sacrifices. He had good values, honesty and hard-work, he respected others, he knew that eventually all this would be rewarded.

That was my foundation and now that I have taken the entrepreneurial leap for myself I carry those values close to me. Yet I also have my own take and it is this......... an entrepreneur must have "Equal parts - tremendous confidence and tremendous fear of failure". It is these two things that make me the business man I am today.

About Paul Lozub

Shortly after Paul graduated from college, his father Ed Kozub passed away, leaving a successful family business behind. Paul's grandfather passed a few years later. On the day his grandfather died, Paul sat in his living room thinking back to the stories he was told about moon-shining during prohibition. As the story goes, his grandfather produced his own vodka during the 1930s and distributed it all over the state of Massachusetts. The entrepreneurial spirit of his father and a business background from years of banking led Paul to ask why small batch vodka wasn't being made today. Paul scoured the internet to learn as much as he could about vodka and spent the next year experimenting with recipes in the basement of his home in Hadley, Massachusetts.

Paul made his first batch of vodka one night in the middle of winter. It became clear that this was his calling in life as he fell in love with every aspect of the vodka making process. Paul made several trips to Poland to perfect his recipe and it was there that he met the master distiller at Polmos Lublin. After several successful meetings the two teamed up to begin crafting the world's most drinkable vodka. V-One is now distilled in Poland by Polmos Lublin, which has been successfully manufacturing its own line of vodka for 100 years. The recipe and the V-One brand are 100% owned by Paul's company Valley Vodka, Inc.

On September 1st 2005 V-One Vodka made its debut in 10 liquor stores and 5 restaurants in Western Massachusetts. The company had no office, no computers, no distributors, just Paul and his V-One Vodka Van.

In the first year, Paul spent all of his time going door to door (bar-to-bar and store-to-store) letting people try his vodka. Many of these restaurant and liquor store owners told Paul V-One was the smoothest vodka they had ever tasted.

From its humble beginnings, V-One Vodka is now considered one of the top vodkas in the world.

Caroline Packman & Lisa Levin-Cohen

FOUNDERS OF PACK HAPPY LLC, WWW.PACKHAPPY.COM

The best advice we ever got was from our respective fathers. Caroline's father always said that successful people adjust to change. That is something that is important to remember when running your own company. We look for the positive in the precarious situations that arise and challenge ourselves to come up with a way to benefit from them.

Lisa's father told us that getting orders is one thing but getting reorders was a sign of true success. We always keep that in mind and work hard to maintain good communication with our vendors to make sure that we get those reorders!

About the Founders

Pack Happy, a designer and manufacturer of chic bags that separate packed items in suitcases. The friends, who met in Los Angeles when Packman worked in fashion and Cohen was a lawyer, started the company in 2001 with dreams of making cute fabric packing bags for items like lingerie, shoes and dirty laundry. "We were both frequent travelers, and we were using baggies and [plastic] bags to pack," says Packman. Today, their products are available online (www.packhappy.com); at high-end retailers like Fred Segal in Santa Monica, California; and in specialty boutiques nationwide.

In 2005 they launched its Baby Happy line of baby products including bibs, blankets and towels.

Scott Matthew
President, Super Fast Pizza

The most important part of your business is the one thing you can't farm out — marketing. You have to learn it yourself. The guys at the ad agencies are only interested in awards, and know almost nothing about getting real people to give YOU real money. (There are experts out there who know how to market, but most of them do it for themselves!)

Read the classics: *Scientific Advertising* by Claude Hopkins, and *Tested Advertising Methods* by John Caples. All the techniques that work were laid out decades ago. Theses include: The Offer; Call to action; Headlines; the Guarantee; Testing. The Ad guys don't know them. Frankly, they couldn't care less. When you fail, they'll just move on to their next sucker. If you want to succeed, YOU have to learn them.

About Scott Matthew

One such night, when an hour seemed too long to wait, Scott went to bed hungry, but woke up inspired.

"If you bake the pizzas in vans on the way to you, it would be so neat. You could probably get it there in 20 minutes," Matthew said.

Matthew jotted down the idea on a Post-it note and incorporated two weeks later. Now his employees roam central Wisconsin in a pair of Super Fast Pizza vans, cooking pizzas in mobile kitchens and delivering them — with the cheese still bubbling when they reach people's doors — in about 15 minutes.

The company uses Mercedes-Benz Sprinters, high-roofed vehicles used as ambulances in Europe that cost about $32,000. For another $65,000 they were outfitted with coolers, five small pizza ovens and touch-screen monitors connected to an Internet-based ordering system staffed by a call center in Nebraska.

Ten types of thin crust pizza such as pepperoni and bacon cheeseburger are made off-site according to Super Fast's specifications and kept cool in refrigerators for a maximum of four days. The pizzas cook in seven to 11 minutes in 600-degree Fahrenheit ovens. That is hotter than average, but workable with the right ingredients and care, said Ostrander.

The results are a cross between a supermarket-bought frozen pizza, a delivery from a chain like Domino's and eating at a pizzeria where the pie comes straight from the oven. They're not for fussy pizza connoisseurs, but will satisfy a quick craving.

Melanie Notkin

Founder and **CEO**, SavvyAuntie.com

The best advice I ever got was to listen to my heart, my body, my mind and my soul. After all, I'm the only one who can hear them.

I had always dreamed of becoming an entrepreneur and had interesting ideas along the way, but nothing my gut told me was the right one. Then on a sunny day in the summer of 2007, I had the idea! Based on my own experience as an aunt, I was going to develop the first online community for women like me - the 50% of American women who are not moms but who love and indulge the children in their lives. Once I became determined, I stopped listening to the people who politely cautioned me against fulfilling my dream.

I listened to myself. And I succeeded.

About Melanie Notkin

Melanie Notkin is America's premier Savvy Auntie, empowering the nearly 50% of American women who are not moms to celebrate all they do for the children in their lives, while living their own lives to the fullest. She launched SavvyAuntie.com, the first online community for aunts and godmothers, in the summer of 2008 to wide-acclaim. The website includes expert content designed specifically for aunts, activities, community and trendy gift ideas.

Melanie identified this influential segment of women, which she has dubbed PANKs (Professional Aunts No Kids), when she herself became an aunt. In February 2009, she guest posted for Lisa Belkin's parenting blog in The New York Times to explain the value of aunts and godmothers in family life. The term has also appeared in *More Magazine, TrendCentral.com, Washington Post, The Record, The Star Ledger, Dallas Morning News* among others. On July 26, 2009, she launched Savvy Auntie's Day, the first national holiday to honor aunts and aunthood.

As tastemaker, Auntie Melanie has been featured numerous times on NBC, CBS and BetterTV.com showcasing the coolest toys of the season. She was also contributing editor at Toy Wishes Magazine.

She has worked with sponsors including leading kid brands like Hasbro, Disney, Yoplait Kids, Sprout, Scholastic, and brands for women including Warner Brothers Sex and the City Movie Download, Turner Networks/TNT, and fashion sites like BeyondTheRack.com and BareNecessities.com. Her groundbreaking and effective advertising campaigns have been featured in Mashable.com, *The New York Times* and *The Wall Street Journal* where she's been lauded as a 'trusted source' and spokesperson for America's top brands.

SavvyAuntie.com was 2009 Webby Award nominee for Best Family/Parenting site and is a Springwise.com Top 10 Lifestyle and Leisure Business Idea for 2008. Melanie is featured on Mashable.com's list of top 5 start ups in New York City's social media hub.

As a successful business woman, she's a weekly panelist on FOX News Strategy Room Business Hour and lectures at various conferences inspiring women, students and entrepreneurs on launching the business of their dreams. She's been featured on First30Days.com, Business Week and Huffington Post for her leveraging of social media to launch and grow her business. She has documented the launch of her own business at her 'auntpreneurial' blog at blog.savvyauntie.com.

Before developing Savvy Auntie, Melanie was an interactive marketing and communications executive for global Fortune 500 companies, including New York Times Digital and American Express, as well as L'Oréal. She is a graduate of McGill University in Montreal, Canada where she was born.

She is a Savvy Auntie and Auntie by Relation (ABR) to a number of wonderful children who are the loves of her life. She is also an Auntie By Choice (ABC) to all of her friends' kids, who come in a very close second. Melanie resides in New York where she is surrounded by the very best the City has to offer.

Andrew Fox

CEO, TRACK ENTERTAINMENT

The best advice I've ever been given is from my mother. She told me to never, ever give up. Ultimately, if you're working harder than the next guy, you will prevail. It might take longer. It might come at the expense of short-term financial gain. And you might not be popular while you're doing it. But if you truly believe that what you're doing is right, it doesn't matter what anyone else says or does.

Love what you do. And if you own your own business, surround yourself with people who love what they do. At Track Entertainment, I feel that everyone here is an extension of my personality. They all work hard. They love what they do. That's what you need as an entrepreneur.

Just like in sports, life is a game of inches. That means you have to play the game like every second is the last second. Keeping with the sports analogy, I wasn't the fastest athlete.

Or the strongest. But I worked harder than anybody else, and eventually I was the captain of my soccer team.

If you're willing to have that kind of commitment, just like the phoenix you can rise from the ashes. I'm a dot-com survivor. After the fallout from the dot-com bust, I nearly lost everything. But I kept working hard. I never gave up on myself, and I never gave up on Clubplanet.com. And here we are today, the internet's leading nightlife resource.

About Andew Fox

Andrew has spent the last 6 years running entertainment and service companies. Andrew is currently CEO of Track Entertainment. In addition, he is also the co-founder and Chairman of ClubPlanet, Inc., the largest and most comprehensive nightlife web destination on the Internet, which provides content, listings, tickets and many other features for nightlife events in over 35 cities around the world.

Until recently, he was also CEO of Way Communications, a national Internet service provider. In 2000, Way Communications was acquired by Frontline Communications Corporation. Andrew was also a partner in Tumble Interactive,a web design firm, which was sold in 1999. In 2000, Andrew founded 3-G Communications, a wireless communications business, which finances and leases cellular towers in North America.

In addition, Andrew is a member of the executive committee of the Ad Club of New York and Director of the New York chapter of Chair Scholars Foundation, Inc., a national non-profit organization which provides scholarships to children and adolescents with disabilities.

Lisa Druxman
FOUNDER AND CEO OF STROLLER STRIDES

The best advice I was ever given was to find something that I have a passion for. When you're an entrepreneur, you are always working. The only way to stay driven and motivated is if you're passionate about what you're doing. Other GREAT advice that I was given...One, when creating your budget, always double your expenses and halve your revenue. If it still shows a profit, you'll be in good shape. Two, create a logo that has no more than two colors so it won't cost you a fortune in screen charges for letterhead, logo gear, etc. I didn't listen to that one and still pay the price with a very colorful logo! Three, stay very focused on WHY you are in this business. For me, it was 100% so that I could be in control of how much time I spent with my children and could work from home. I wanted to be a mom first and foremost but couldn't accomplish that in any other job. When I start to get pulled in many directions for the business, I go back to that reason for being in it and the rest just falls in to place. And last but not least, the best advice I was ever given came from my parents. They told me that I could be anything and do anything that I ever wanted if I would just work hard at it. And they were right!

About Lisa Druxman

Lisa Druxman, M.A., the creator of Stroller Strides has been in the fitness industry since 1990. Lisa Druxman received her Master's degree at San Diego State University in Psychology with an emphasis in Exercise Adherence and Weight Control.

While there, she worked with their weight control clinic and has since become a certified and published educator in this field. She created a weight management program called L.E.A.N. (Learn Eating Awareness and Nutrition) which has been offered at exclusive health clubs such as The Sporting Club at Aventine in La Jolla.

She has worked as a group exercise instructor, personal trainer and club manager at some of the country's finest health clubs. She has lectured and taught at renowned spas such as The Golden Door and Rancho La Puerta. But it wasn't until she became a mom herself that she realized the need for specialty "mom" fitness. As soon as Lisa's son was born, she got outside with her stroller. Not having the time to get back to the gym, she created a series of exercises to get her back in shape. Before you knew it, a new workout was born! Now, moms all over the country are getting a chance to Stroller Stride!

Ira Bryck,
DIRECTOR, UMASS FAMILY BUSINESS CENTER

In a previous life chapter, I co-operated my family's 4th generation childrenswear store with my parents (oldest in the nation [the store, not the parents]). As Yogi Berra would say, I learned a lot just from watching. My father taught me at a young age (3) that customer satisfaction was all about listening-discover what the customer really wants and deliver it. But often customers doesn't really know what they want. The best they might come up with as an explanation is "I'll know it when I see it." So you really have to tune in to that customer, to unearth his taste, her fear, what they are really looking to accomplish by choosing the designer label over the identical but unbranded suit, the simple but elegant Christening dress over the flashy but inexpensive one. Customer satisfaction relies on your customer empathy at that point, so that the "wow" you deliver might be that you understand that buyer more than she understands herself. On the other hand, my mother had an expression: "If everyone leaves with something, you're overstocked." She knew that though we needed to be wide and deep in inventory, we made 80% of our sales on 20% of our items. We could go out of business trying to please everyone. If we're all things to all people, we're really nothing to anybody. Though I no longer sell suits and dresses, and my current business is delivering "knowledge, experience, honesty and wisdom" to business owning families, hardly a day passes that I don't implement those lessons from my mom and dad.

About Ira Bryck

Ira Bryck is Director of the UMass Family Business Center at UMass Amherst Continuing & Professional Education. The center provides a noncommercial, interactive learning community for business families in Western New England and beyond. Ira and the center also produce the family business newsletter Related Matters, web site www.umass.edu/fambiz and advice column, Dear Ira: Fresh Air and Cold Water for the Perplexed Business Family, and confers on an array of family business challenges. Ira is the author of three plays about life in family business, presented as "edu-tainment" to forums of business families. His third play, "A Tough Nut to Crack", is based on his 17 years in his family's 4th generation childrenswear business on Long Island, where he served simultaneously in every role from president to tailor.

Marissa Shipman

CEO AND FOUNDER OF THEBALM (WWW.THEBALM.COM)

The best advice I ever got was to not let fear get in my way of going for the gold. As Murphy's Law implies something will always go wrong when you least expect it. Obstacles are inevitable, and anyone who tells you differently is just plain lying.

When I first started my business, there were many occasions where I felt like quitting. I asked myself time and time again if what I was doing was feasible. Then one day, my best friend, Carla, handed me a quote that changed the way I view everything.

"Far better it is to dare mighty things, to win glorious triumphs even though checkered by failure, than to rank with those poor spirits who neither enjoy nor suffer much because they live in the gray twilight that knows neither victory nor defeat."

It wasn't soon after that I was flashed with inspiration... if you live your life within the boundaries circumscribed by others, you'll never know the full scope of your potential—nor will anyone else.

Today, Theodore Roosevelt's mantra is something to which I frequently refer and share with others.

About Marissa Shipman

Marissa realized that there were a few simple products she needed to help her feel glam all the time. Then she decided that if she needed them, other women probably did too.

So she went to Amazon, bought 11 books on how to make makeup and started mixing in her kitchen. "I went crazy. I had a web site designed, got incorporated, worked out a budget, and hired a chemist." And the rest is history! Well, not yet but with her great ingredients, gorgeous colors and fabulous scents, Marissa is certainly making makeup history.

Marissa has a Bachelor of Arts from Tulane University. Through her Theater Arts major and career in television production, Marissa developed keen insights into present day American pop culture that enhance her understanding of cosmetic trends. Marissa is glamorous and fun and her personality definitely shows through in her products.

Vadim Kotelnikov

FOUNDER, TEN3 BUSINESS E-COACH – INNOVATION UNLIMITED,
WWW.1000VENTURES.COM

The best advice I ever got was very simple. My Friend, Veronika Makhina, advised me to learn Microsoft's FrontPage, a web design software. I faced a big problem at that time. I wished to develop the first-ever business e-coach helping people build their entrepreneurial creativity. I developed an initial content for it and hired a web-design firm to build a web site. They built it, but it didn't meet my expectations. I hired another firm, but they were not able to produce the product I wanted either. The story was the same with the third web design firm. I realized that the communication gap between me and the web designers was too big. The innovative concept of e-coach was too difficult and complex for them to understand. The advice of Veronika was timely and practical. She had learned FrontPage and designed her web site herself within a week. I've got excited about the idea and started learning web design. The more I learned about web design, the more ideas I had about developing the e-Coach concept.

I launched Ten3 Business e-Coach with initial investment of just US$1,000. Within two years it became the global leader in its market niche. We had customers in 68 countries and offices in seven countries.

About Vadim Kotelnikov

Vadim is an inventor, author and founder of Ten3 Business e-Coach – Inspiration, Innovation, and Growth Unlimited!

Ten3 Business e-Coach is the World's #1 – and actually the only! – inspirational business e-coaching resource for modern business leaders, venturepreneurs, innovators, business consultants, and trainers. It inspires entrepreneurial creativity and leadership, facilitates systems thinking, and helps you discover innovative business synergies. Over 10,000 people from all over the World visit the free version of Ten3 Business e-Coach every day.

Vadim Kotelnikov has been providing international business consultancy and training services since 1990. He has worked in 50+ countries. He holds Scientific Degrees in MSc Cybernetics, MSc Economics, PhD Economics.

Michael Jansma

FOUNDER AND PRESIDENT OF WWW.GEMAFFAIR.COM

The best advice I ever received was from my college finance teacher. My class was having a discussion about significance of company profits. We were learning about the practicality or commonality of companies existing, while not making money. This was baffling to me.

"Cash flow is <u>always</u> the factor that determines whether or not a company can exist, regardless of profits," he said. *"The lifeblood of business,"* he further explained.

He stated that cash flow played the same role as the blood in our bodies. No blood, no life. He provided us with many real life examples, showing us companies who for years spent previous years' profits, leveraged employee retirement funds, borrowed money from banks and vendors, and remained in business, despite having no profit. Eventually, many of these companies turned around and became profitable. He also showed us real life examples of companies where profits were exorbitant, yet lack of cash flow killed the company. Extending credit to customers and having huge Accounts Receivable eventually drove the company out of business. They were unable to pay their vendors and their employees.

I experienced this first hand a year ago when my company suddenly lost one of its largest vendors. We were unprepared, since we had never really sought other large sources of revenue. We had outstanding bills from vendors and not much revenue; keeping the lights on became very difficult. Suddenly, I painfully remembered my professor's words. I did what those other companies did: I borrowed. And borrowed. And got back to work. Fortunately today, we are profitable. Managing cash flow is the top priority of my job.

About Michael Jansma

Michael Jansma established GEMaffair.com in 1996. The company specializes in fine jewelry, watches, and accessories for both men and women. The site, which is hosted by Amazon. com, has completed more than 20 million in jewelry sales online. In 2005, the company added watches to its already expansive inventory and became a certified Bulova watches merchant. The company's also sells directly to consumers on third party sites such as Amazon and Ebay among others.

In 2009 announced they would now offer clients professional third party appraisals on any item purchased from their online store. The ecommerce retailer is one of the web's largest colored gemstone jewelry providers with over 7,500 unique items in their webstore.

John Jansheski
President and CEO, DenTek Oral Care

The best advice I ever received in business is: There is no such thing as a free lunch. Tom Elliott was the President of Washington Fish & Oyster and also one of my mentors. Mr. Elliott afforded my burgeoning company the use of his Telex machine to communicate with Korea. When our manufacturer's quote for freight "prepaid" which means Freight On Board delivered to my warehouse noted that the cost for FOB shipping would be "free," Tom warned me that when you are in business, there are very few things a company does not pay for one way or another. I received this eminent advice from Tom in 1984. It has served our company well for over two decades. "No free lunch" prompts us to look at every deal and examine it for hidden costs and charges. We make sure we are getting the best possible price for goods and services.

About John Jansheski

John Jansheski Founded DenTek Oral Care, Inc., in 1982 and serves as its Chief Executive Officer and Chief Innovation Officer.

DenTek® was founded by John Jansheski in Petaluma, California and relocated to Maryville, Tennessee in 2001. He remains CEO today. Since its inception, DenTek® has focused on providing innovative oral care products for professionals and consumers. The company began with the Dental Pik™, and now offers over 25 products designed for health care professionals and oral health zealots. DenTek' products go beyond brushing and provide solutions for flossing, braces care, teeth grinding, jaw pain and much more. As the spirit of innovation and dental hygiene fever continues to drive the company, DenTek leads the way in providing fresh, innovative solutions to meet the needs of oral health conscious consumers. DenTek products can be purchased at major retailers across the country. DenTek offers a full-line of oral care products helping you to be your healthiest.

Jonah Staw
CEO, Miss Matched, Inc.

When I was 21 and working my first job out of college, Harvey the Chairman of the company I worked for took me out for lunch and said "Jonah, the key to business is never learning how to do the things you don't want to do." I laughed at the time, because all I was doing was menial tasks.

As an entrepreneur, you have to 'do' everything. As the CEO of Miss Matched, Inc., I meet with other business leaders in boardrooms and travel the world cutting deals, but at the same time, I answer customer emails and even stuff envelopes.

However, the key to Harvey's advise is that if you don't want to do something, there is bound to be someone out there that can do it better, cheaper, and faster.

For me, the key to being a successful entrepreneur is being true to who I am and what I am good at. As a business we also must do the same. What does Miss Matched Inc do? We design, market and sell products. Period. We don't warehouse them. We don't fabricate them. We don't ship them....We do the stuff we are good at and and leave all the rest to the experts.

This has been the key to our success at selling mismatched socks sold in odd numbers.

About Johan Shaw

Johan Shaw always had an entrepreneurial spirit. At age 8, Mr. Staw started his own postcard company, drawing birdlike images on special paper to sell at local bookstores in Berkeley, Calif.

"As an 8-year-old, you're rolling in dough if you can buy an extra pack of Now and Later candy," he says.

After an early career as an architect he designed and built his own dream house and a stint at design firm Frog, Mr. Staw launched Miss Matched in 2004.

The quirky sock company has since expanded to pajamas and bedroom furniture and has an upcoming apparel line for tweens. Last year, revenue jumped 28% from 2007, to $32 million, and Mr. Staw says e-commerce sales grew 80%. The brand is carried at Macy's, FAO Schwarz, Bed Bath & Beyond and at 3,000 specialty shops.

But that's not the endgame. Despite the recession's chilling effect on retail, Mr. Staw plans to open a store in Grand Central Terminal this spring and is searching for another location. The expansion is part of a business plan underwritten by private equity firm Catterton Partners.

Julie Mierau

PRESIDENT, JM COMMUNICATIONS, INC.

My father spent 35 years working in a factory to support our family. His advice to us was never to stay in a job you hate; you'll be miserable, and the company won't take care of you in the end. So when I quit my last full-time job to open a freelance writing and consulting business, he was my biggest fan. There are myriad ways to make a living, including being self-employed or opening a business. Make sure you investigate all of them to find where you best fit in the world of work.

About Julie Mierau

Julie serves as the director of Entrepreneurial Education & Training at Iowa Western Community College. She works with educators to develop entrepreneurial curriculum for students in K-12 and the community college level. She coordinates training programs for business owners, including FastTrac classes, networking events and specialized training. Julie co-owns The Cornerstone Mansion, Omaha's only historic inn, and formerly owned JM Communications, a freelance writing and public relations consulting firm.

Mario Morino
CHAIRMAN, VENTURE PHILANTHROPY PARTNERS

The best advice came from my business partner and his nuggets of wisdom were

First, the twin thieves of success are "ego" and "greed," for they ruin more businesses and wreck more lives than anything else. Deal with these as you see success, and you will really be successful!

Second, it's all about focus and execution...ideas are great, strategy is wonderful and necessary, but if you don't do the boring "blocking and tackling" day in and day out, you won't make it.

Third, always remember who's buying and who's selling, and be sure to remind the accountants and the lawyers that it's YOUR business and they are advisors, not owners.

And fourth, remember that no one is so good that luck doesn't matter...work hard, stay smart, and be lucky! When you succeed, don't be pompous, and don't forget that good fortune helped you along the way.

About Mario Morino

Mario Morino is co-founder and chairman of Venture Philanthropy Partners and chairman of the Morino Institute.

His career spans more than 40 years as entrepreneur, technologist, and civic and business leader. He also has a long history of civic engagement and philanthropy in the National Capital Region and more recently in Northeast Ohio.

In the early 1970s, Mario co-founded and helped build the Legent Corporation, a software and services firm that became a market leader and one of the industry's 10 largest firms by the early 1990s. He retired from the private sector in 1992 and, since then, his focus has been almost exclusively in the nonprofit sector.

Mario's current private sector work is limited to his affiliation with General Atlantic LLC, one of the leading global growth equity firms providing capital for companies in markets with high growth potential, typically driven by globalization, industry consolidation, technology, demographics, liberalized markets and other transformative factors. He has been associated with the firm for more than 20 years, initially as its second investment in 1983, later as a Special Advisor, and now as a member of its Executive Advisory Board.

In his philanthropic work, Mario founded the Morino Institute in 1994 to stimulate innovation and entrepreneurship, advance a more effective philanthropy, close social divides, and understand the relationship and impact of the Internet on our society. In the 1990s, his efforts focused on the application of the Internet in communities and, in particular, opening up new technology-enabled learning opportunities and centers for children and youth of low-income families. Concurrently, he played a leadership role helping the National Capital Region understand and advance its position as a world center in information technology and telecommunications.

In 2000, Mario co-founded Venture Philanthropy Partners as a philanthropic investment organization that concentrates investments of money, expertise, and contacts to improve the lives and boost the opportunities of children of low-income families in the National Capital Region. He has been one of the leaders in adapting the relevant principles of venture and growth equity investment firms and applying them for investing in the nonprofit sector to build stronger, high-impact, lasting nonprofit institutions. He also helped bring together and continues to advance a growing community of high net worth donors in and around the nation's capital.

In addition to his roles with Venture Philanthropy Partners and the Morino Institute, Mario serves as a member of the board of trustees of The Cleveland Clinic Foundation, an honorary trustee of The Brookings Institution, an Emeritus Trustee of Case Western Reserve University, and on the boards of the Lawrence School and Saint Joseph Academy. He is a special advisor to Echoing Green; a member of the PEACE X PEACE advisory council; a member of the advisory board for the Center for the Advancement of Social Entrepreneurship (CASE), The Fuqua School of Business, Duke University; and a member of the Board of Governors of the Partnership for Public Service. He also informally advises scores of organizations and individuals across a range of areas.

An active public speaker and writer, Mario has been the recipient of numerous awards and honors. He received a B.B.A. from Case Western Reserve University and lives in greater Cleveland, Ohio, with his wife and three children.

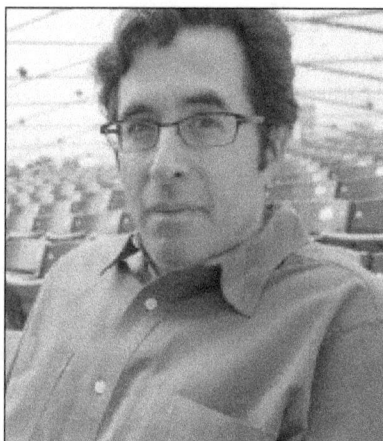

Barry Moltz

SERIAL ENTREPRENEUR, AUTHOR AND ANGEL INVESTOR

When I was leaving IBM, Tom Lietag told me that I was a pretty good business person. But I would be a better business person when I had failed. At IBM, all I did was succeed. I thought he was jealous. I did not realize that he was foretelling my future for the next 5 years as I was fired from my next job and went out of business in my first start up.

I learned it's okay to be afraid of failure, but I should go ahead and do it anyway. I also learned humility. Businesses turn quickly. I share my success when things go well. I give myself a break when things go badly.

About Barry Moltz

Barry Moltz has founded and run small businesses with a great deal of success and failure for more than 15 years.

After successfully selling his last operating business, Barry has branched out into a number of entrepreneurship-related activities. He founded an angel investor group, an angel fund, and is a former advisory member of the board of the Angel Capital Education Foundation.

His first book, *You Need to Be A Little Crazy: The Truth about Starting and Growing Your Business*, describes the ups and downs and emotional trials of running a business. It is in its fourth reprint and has been translated into Chinese, Russian, Korean and Thai. His second book, *Bounce! Failure, Resiliency and the Confidence to Achieve Your Next Great Success*, shows what it takes to comeback and develop true business confidence. His third book due out this fall is called, *BAM! Delivering Customer Service in a Self-Service World*.

Barry is a nationally recognized expert on entrepreneurship who has given hundreds of presentations to audiences ranging from 20 to 20,000. He was appointed by the Illinois Governor in 2005 to serve as Chairman of the board of the Institute for Entrepreneurship Education (IIEE). As a member of the Entrepreneurship Hall of Fame, he also has taught entrepreneurship as an adjunct professor at the Illinois Institute of Technology. He has appeared on many TV and radio programs such as The Big Idea with Donny Deutsch and The Tavis Smiley Show.

James A. Warner

PUBLISHER, SHORE PUBLISHING NEWSPAPERS

Early in my career one of clients said, "Sales reps are the life blood of your company. Each sales rep is unique and special." His words had a big impact on me. Through experience I've learned that the superstar sales rep expects to be treated differently and a good manager will cater to that. It isn't playing favoritism; it is managing them on a personal level. I try to address the individual needs of each of my sales reps. I've learned that if I need to cut costs the worst thing I can do is reduce a sales rep's income or benefits to save money.

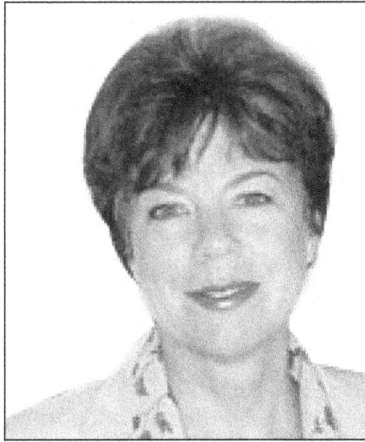

Susan Bilney

FOUNDER AND PRESIDENT, WOMEN'S ADVANTAGE

Many of us have read or heard from others what Michael Gerber has to say in his book *The E-Myth Revisited* about being an entrepreneur. That is, we not only need to work *in* our business, doing the activity for which people hire us, but we also need to work *on* our business, which includes all the rest....the marketing, customer service, finance, etc. However, understanding that we need to work on these other activities is still not enough because if we hate doing them we are not going to do them well, or do a good job of managing others who do them. Therefore, the best advice I heard had to do with making a shift in our thinking. We need to find a way to *love* working on our business, or at least like it. Only then will the work we do on these activities be truly effective…as well as being relatively effortless!

An example of this idea in practice would be my own progression towards enjoying networking events with other business owners. In the beginning, when thinking about attending one of these meetings my self-talk went something like, "I'm an introvert…I'm terrible at networking…I'm not a joiner…I've got better things to do with my time." It is not surprising then that I found it difficult to get myself to networking events and that I did not enjoy myself once I was there. Once I realized how counter-productive this self-talk was, I started looking for ways to shift my thinking and make networking fun.

The first thing I did was to stop identifying myself as an introvert. I knew I had the requisite skills for meeting and talking intelligently with strangers even though it wasn't my favorite thing to do. Then I looked for a positive way of viewing these networking events. I recognized that because I quit working at an organization and started my own business in my home, the likelihood that my social world would shrink was high. Since expanding my world was more of what I had in mind I knew I would need ways of reaching out to others. Networking with other women business owners was the perfect vehicle for connecting with like-minded people who would understand what I was going through.

I also realized that if I joined the board or one of the committees in these networking groups, the likelihood that I would attend their events would increase. In the process of becoming more involved with these organizations, I shifted from the role of being a "guest" at the meetings to assuming the role of "host," welcoming and introducing members and guests to one another. The result was that I began to feel like I belonged, which led me to be more relaxed and to really connect with others in a way that has resulted in not only new business relationships but also new friendships. I now look forward to these events… something I never thought possible.

The evolution in my thinking and behavior which allowed me to go from hating networking events to enjoying them may seem fairly obvious. However, take it from someone whose personality tests place her near the end of the introvert scale, this shift is no small thing. It was the starting place for my understanding that I could possibly love…and be effective in…other areas of marketing, as well as in the other areas of my business.

About Susan Bilney

Susan Bilney brings over 20 years of experience in business management and personal development to her career as a professional coach. Working in a broad range of business industries and environments, she has held executive and management level positions including Vice President of Operations for a telecommunications company, Operations Manager/Marketing for a small business communications company, and Administrative Manager for a non-profit organization serving at-risk teens.

In addition to her active business career, Susan has completed a Bachelor of Arts degree in Psychology and a Master's Degree in Life Skills Education at Sonoma State University. Her combined Master's program integrated the disciplines of psychology and education with an objective of developing proficiency in teaching life skills to adults of all ages.

While completing her coursework, Susan was invited to be a university instructor at Sonoma State University. She developed and taught a curriculum in Relationship Skills for university level students. Soon after, she chose professional coaching as her life direction so she could utilize her skills to help other women shape the professional and personal lives they truly wanted.

Susan is now the successful owner of Women's Advantage, a coaching business which focuses on helping women make significant transitions in their professional lives. Susan brings a unique understanding of women's challenges to her business based on years of experience as a business manager and as a mentor to others seeking to transform an unsatisfying career.

A graduate of Coach U., one of the leading and oldest accredited coaching schools in the U.S., Susan is also a member of the International Coaching Federation, the local chapter of the National Association of Female Executives (NAFE), Toastmasters, the National Organization of Women Business Owners (NAWBO), the American Association of University Women (AAUW) and her local chamber of commerce.

She is an active participant in A Hand-Up Coaching (AHUC), a non-profit organization working with low-income women in their professional lives. AHUC operates in conjunction with the national organization Dress for Success.

Susan has also volunteered her coaching services to events such as the "Women Seeing Beyond Today" conference, which facilitates the empowerment of women and provides opportunities for strengthening women's communities.

Norman Love

FOUNDER AND **CEO**, NORMAN LOVE CONFECTIONS

Mr. Horst Schulte, former CEO of the Ritz-Carlton Company, told me to go to work with a purpose, to go to work striving to be excellent everyday. In fact, to go to work to be better than you were yesterday. This is our philosophy, my employees and I, and has been since day one.

About Norman Love

Norman Love's lifelong passion for fine art and fine foods has propelled him to the very heights of the culinary world.

During his 13 years as corporate executive pastry chef for The Ritz-Carlton company, Love opened hotel pastry kitchens in such diverse locales as Boston, Dubai and Bali. Indeed, his avant-garde artistry has influenced signature desserts served at Ritz-Carlton hotels worldwide.

Love's fascination with food began during his childhood in Philadelphia, where he spent hours working in the kitchen with his mother and grandmother. "I always had a desire to create art and could relate art with food," he said. "And, of course, my favorite ingredient was chocolate."

Love honed his talents with two years of work and study in a private pastry shop in southern France, followed by jobs as executive pastry chef for The Ritz-Carlton hotels in Naples, Florida, and St. Louis, Missouri, and the famed Beverly Hills Hotel in Beverly Hills, California. He was just 30 years old when The Ritz named him to oversee its worldwide corps of pastry chefs.

What followed were 13 years of stellar accomplishments and international acclaim. Chocolatier and Pastry Art and Design magazines named him one of the country's top 10 pastry chefs in 1996 and 1997. In 1999, he led the U.S. team to a bronze medal in the biennial Coup du Monde de la Patisserie (World Cup of Pastry) competition in Lyons, France, which featured the top pastry chefs from 18 nations.

He was among 18 chefs chosen to make a birthday cake at the 150th Smithsonian Anniversary Celebration in Washington, D.C., and one of only 26 selected to appear on the 39-part series "Baking with Julia," which aired on public television. He's made numerous appearances on the Discovery Channel's "Great Chefs"; series and his desserts have graced the covers of Art Culinaire, Bakery Magazine and other prominent culinary publications. He is also co-founder of the National Pastry Team Championship .

Love left The Ritz in 2001 to found Norman Love Confections, formerly Ganache Chocolates. It wasn't long before the accolades began pouring in. In February, 2002, USA Today named Norman Love Confections, formerly Ganache Chocolates, one of the top 10 artisan chocolate companies in the country.

Isabel Isidro
Vice President, PowerHomeBiz.com LLC

The best advice I ever received in entrepreneurship came from my own experience.

In my late teens, I decided to open a video rental shop because I spend so much time and money watching movies. Movies were my passion, and I typically watched 2-4 movies a day. Instead of giving the rental money to somebody else, I figured I might as well open my own video rental store.

I make decisions fast, and in a week's time I was applying for my permits and licenses, buying inventory and looking for a location. In less than a month's time, my store was up and running. But I knew next to nothing about the video business. Only later did I find out that the video rental business is a low-margin, high volume and inventory intensive business. Worse, the location I got did not provide the demand that I needed.

The business proved to be a huge drain on my resources (money was coming out instead of coming in!). I was able to eventually turn it around when I tapped new markets and introduced a video rental program for corporate workers that proved to be such a hit.

The whole experience was a crash course on what to do and what not to do in entrepreneurship that still rings true today. I learned everything from that experience, from marketing, record keeping, managing employees, accounting, customer service, etc. Most of all, I learned things about myself, and what I can do, which proved to be extremely invaluable.

The main lesson for me is that passion should go hand in hand with knowledge when starting a business. Being passionate about what you do is not enough; you need to know what you are getting into and be prepared for everything that comes with it. Passion will keep you going, but knowledge will steer you in the right direction.

About Isabel Isidro

Isabel Isidro is the Managing Editor of PowerHomeBiz.com LLC, an online magazine for starting, running, managing and marketing a home-based business.

Maxine Clark

FOUNDER AND CHIEF EXECUTIVE BEAR,
BUILD-A-BEAR WORKSHOP

Use your experience. Be prepared for the unexpected and keep your eyes open to the possibilities of what you can imagine. As an entrepreneur it is part of your job to bring energy and new ideas to the work place—keep thinking out of the box.

About Maxine Clark

Maxine Clark is one of the true innovators in the retail industry. During her 30-year career, her ability to spot emerging retail and merchandising trends and her insight into the desires of the American consumer have generated growth for retail leaders, including department store, discount and specialty stores. In 1997, she founded Build-A-Bear Workshop, a teddy-bear themed retail-entertainment experience. Today there are more than 400 Build-A-Bear Workshop stores worldwide, including company-owned stores in the U.S., Puerto Rico, Canada, the United Kingdom, Ireland and France, and franchise stores in

Europe, Asia, Australia and Africa. Build-A-Bear Workshop extended its in-store interactive experience online in 2007 with the launch of its virtual world at buildabearville.com®

In 2008, Maxine Clark was named one of The 25 Most Influential People in Retailing by Chain Store Age; in 2006, she was inducted into the Junior Achievement National Business Hall of Fame and received the 2006 Luminary Award for Entrepreneurial Achievement from the Committee of 200. She was named a Customer-Centered Leader in the 2005 Customer First Awards by Fast Company. Maxine was named one of the Wonder Women of Toys by Playthings magazine and Women in Toys, and was also one of the National Finalists in Retail for the Ernst & Young Entrepreneur of the Year 2004. Build-A-Bear Workshop® was named to the 2009 FORTUNE Best Companies to Work For® list. Buildabearville.com received a 2009 'Best of the Web' award from WiredSafety at the 9th Annual Wired Kids Summit and a 2008 Excellent Product iParenting Media Award. In 2005, the National Association of Small Business Investment Companies made Build-A-Bear Workshop Portfolio Company of the Year; it was named one of the International Council of Shopping Centers "Hottest Retailers of 2004" and the Retail Innovator of the Year for 2001 by The National Retail Federation.

Maxine is a member of the Board of Directors of The J.C. Penney Company, Inc., and serves on the Board of Trustees of Washington University in St. Louis. She is Chair of Teach For America – St. Louis and a member of the Teach For America National Board. She is a member of the KETC Channel 9 – PBS Board of Directors and on the National Children's Museum's Board of Trustees. She is also a member of the Committee of 200. Maxine is a graduate of the University of Georgia, and holds an Honorary Doctor of Laws degree from St. Louis University. In 2006, she published her first book "The Bear Necessities of Business: Building a Company with Heart".

Bill Thomas
President, Thomas Coaching Institute

During my first year of coaching full time, I was working with a client on the phone in another state, who was building a coaching practice. I noticed on his website he had earned a 2nd degree black belt in a martial art called Aikido. I have always been a fan of the martial arts, and begin to ask him questions about Aikido. Knowing my Coaching specialty was leadership he advised me to make a commitment to Aikido. He called again after our coaching session to inform me that he had reviewed the dojo's (where Martial Arts are practiced) in my area (San Antonio, TX) and three dojos were within 2-5 miles from my home. Also, they were only four dojos in our city. I called all three and joined one of them within a week. Today I'm a Sho-Dan. (Black Belt) All of the movements in Aikido are win-win, and, Aikido has NO offense. It is often referred to as the Gentle Marital Art. Later, John O'Neil wrote a book called Leadership Aikido, I believe I have read it 20 times. I have been using the wonderful principles for several years as I Coach Executives at all levels, Aikdio has taken my Coaching to a much higher level and has benefited many Executives over the last 10 years. Demonstrating the Randori Principles (Testing for the black belt) be in the right place, with the right technique, at the right time, with the right level of power. Which might mean: Location-product/service-timing-leverage (vision, mission, purpose) Oh, by the way, that is WIN-WIN.

About Bill Thomas

Born and raised in Indianapolis, Indiana, today I am a Personal & Business Coach residing in Springfield, Illinois. Through the direction of a great Mentor Coach Sandy Vilas, I have built a successful Business, The Thomas Coaching Institute. In June of 1998, my business was recognized by the San Antonio, Texas Chamber of Commerce as The Outstanding Business Leader of the year!!

In July 1998, I formed a strategic alliance with another excellent coach and started a new corporation named Coach Squared, C2. We focus on the Fortune Five Hundred Corporations and design programs to meet their needs.

My clients are Business Owners/Entrepreneurs, CEO's, Professionals, i.e., Medical and Dental Practices, Sales & Marketing, etc. Also, people in Transition, wanting to start a new business, or a Coaching practice. What I do best is assist my clients in obtaining a bigger, better, happier, healthier, and wealthier tomorrow, today!

CLIENT LIST: M&G Polymers (West VA), Ford Motor Credit, VIA Metropolitan Transit, Drash Consulting Engineers, Guido Lumber Company, Hopstar Medical management, Xanadu Orchids, Methodist Hospital System, KMOL News San Antonio, and 181 individuals starting a new business.

Ryan P. M. Allis
CEO, Broadwick Corp

The best advice I have ever received is to have a bias toward action. I see many prospective entrepreneurs who have an idea but never get moving on it. They spend months perfecting their business plans but can never make the break and take the first steps. In trying to help young entrepreneurs get over this hurdle I like to relate an anecdote. Imagine you are at your friend's house and want to get back to your house which is four miles away. You can either stay at your friends house until all the traffic lights along the way are green and then leave, or you can start now. Although you'll run into a few stops along the way, you'll make it to your destination a lot quicker than if you waited for everything to be perfect. Have a bias toward action and get going. You may not know all the steps or the problems you'll run into, but that is okay. As you progress toward your goal, you will continue faster and faster up the learning curve. As you move forward you'll gain new knowledge and build new relationships which will be very important in helping you reach your vision.

About Ryan Allis

Ryan is an international speaker, author, and syndicated columnist on the topics of entrepreneurship, email marketing, and search engine optimization. Ryan has been featured on ABC News and in *Investors' Business Daily*, the *Daily Times of India*, *Entrepreneur Magazine, SuccessCoach Magazine, CosmoGirl*, and *Young Money Magazine*, and in 2005 was named by *BusinessWeek* as one of the "Top 25 Entrepreneurs Under 25."

As the founder of the Anti-Poverty Campaign, a non-profit organization, he is dedicated to reducing poverty in developing countries, the Chairman of the Carolina Entrepreneurship Club, and a member of the Raleigh Chapter of the Young Entrepreneurs' Organization.

Kathryn Goetzke White
PRESIDENT AND CEO, INNOVATIVE ANALYSIS, INC.
FOUNDER, IFRED (WWW.IFRED.ORG OR WWW.DEPRESSION.ORG)

Every good idea is challenged and meets resistance. I did not meet one person, in the original concepting of my new product line, who thought it was a good idea and thought I would succeed. Everyone told me I was crazy and it would never work. However, instead of giving up I listened carefully to what they were saying and made 'modifications' to my plans when needed. I didn't quit when I was told I could not get my product in to retailers – I listened as to why the person thought I couldn't, overcame their perceived obstacles through ingenuity, thought, and planning, and eventually succeeded in getting my product line in retailers.

About Kathryn Goetzke White

Kathryn Goetzke, age 37, is the owner and chief Strategist at Innovative Analysis. She is the entrepreneur and innovator behind Mood-lites™, a new category of lighting in the $5 billion dollar U.S. lighting marketplace (it is about time Edison got a makeover!). She is armed with an MBA in International

65

Marketing, an undergraduate degree in Psychology, over fifteen years of experience with small and large, Fortune 100 companies, has managed multiple successful political campaigns, and has created a new nonprofit and brand for depression, being a proud depression survivor and supporter of the disease herself.

Prior to founding her own company, Goetzke, a world traveler who has worked and studied across the world, was Vice President of Sales and Marketing for Compass Marketing. She guided Fortune 100 companies like The Gillette Company, Johnson & Johnson, Unilever, General Mills, and others in development of Alternate Channels, leading revenue growth of over 400% for Compass Marketing. White also led the strategic planning and business development for Brazilian-based Seed Technology Solutions (SeedTS), a Sao Paulo based technology firm, with income rising over 200% and project acquisitions with Deutsche Bank.

Goetzke began her career managing a law firm and then at 3M Corporation where she worked as a Research Manager at their headquarters in Minneapolis. She moved on to develop her experience at American Express serving different capacities in New Products, Marketing, Research and Promotions. After spending four years at American Express she went on to learn the ropes of Advertising in the West, helping small companies take on the big ones, while exploring the mountains, wildlife and confronting grizzlies along the way. Goetzke has a Master of Business Administration degree in International Marketing Management and a Bachelor of Arts degree in Psychology, International Studies and Biology.

In addition to launching Mood-lites, Goetzke started a non-profit organization for depression called iFred (the International Foundation for Research and Education on Depression – www.depression.org) dedicated to 'rebranding' the disease with the color orange and sunflower symbol (similar to how breast cancer used pink/the pink ribbon). For years we have associated hopelessness and helplessness with this disease, when in fact it is very treatable in 80% of cases. According to the World Health Organization, depression is going to be the 2nd leading killer worldwide by the year 2020, this trend is reversible – people just need to feel hopeful enough to get help.

Committed to donating her personal resources to philanthropic causes, Goetzke also served as a board member for the Watson Children's Shelter, and on advisory boards and committees for the United Way, YWCA, Camp Mak-A-Dream, the Breast Cancer Resource Guide, Sailing into the Arts, and the Missoula Food Bank.

Bray J. Brockbank

VICE PRESIDENT, STRATEGIC
MARKETING & BUSINESS DEVELOPMENT, SYSTYX

The best advice I've ever received really wasn't advice so much as an amalgam of advice and example from those closest to me. So, to put this all into words might sound something like this, "A man is literally what he thinks, his character is the sum of all his thoughts, desires, and actions. What a man achieves and all that he fails to achieve is also a direct result of his thoughts, desires, and actions. Thought, desire, and action are the foundation of character." The "thought" is the design and plan, "desire" is the passion and vision, and "action" is the will to make it happen. As I grow older I come to better understand and appreciate this advice more fully. I've tried to follow this advice not only in my professional pursuits as a marketing professional and entrepreneur but also in my personal life.

Dr. Loren Ekroth

WWW.CONVERSATION-MATTERS.COM

The most important guideline I acquired when entrepreneur-ing has been to learn from the best. That is, those other entrepreneurs who have been manifestly successful. Listen to them; read them; model yourself after their best practices. Immerse yourself in the energies of these successful people. On the other hand, pay little attention to those advice-givers and nay-sayers who are neither entrepreneurs nor successful in starting and following through (and there will be many). This group includes some family members, old school friends, and tire-kickers who may be dreamers but never do much. All entrepreneurs, info-preneurs, and mini-preneurs have to be creative and bold and have to take some risks. Spend time with these people and learn from them.

About Loren Ekroth

Loren Ekroth is a speaker, trainer and coach to corporations and government agencies with clients such as Sheraton Hotels, Hawaiian Electric Company, United Way, Naval Training Center Pacific, The Nature Conservancy, City and County of Honolulu, U.S. Army, International Association of Professional Administrators, ASTD Las Vegas, Farm Equipment Manufacturers Association, CUE Financial.

His Business Background includes:

- Founder-director of the Natural Learning Center of Hawaii, a personal development training organization.
- President of Kama'aina Fundraisers, a wholesale product fundraising company for the state of Hawaii.
- Founder, National Better Conversation Week (November)
- Creator of "Conversation Coaching Clubs," a worldwide self-help group for building conversation skills.

Career/Life Counselor:

- Business and personal coach: 30 years experience helping people achieve greater competence and success.

Writer:

- 100+ columns on interpersonal relations for the Sunday Honolulu Advertiser, the Hawaii state newspaper
- 300+ electronic articles in "Better Conversations" ezine
- Forthcoming book, "Conversation: A Self-Coaching Guide." late fall 2007.

Education:

- Ph.D., University of Minnesota, Intercultural Communication
- Global travel to 85 countries, instructional and research work in France, Germany, Italy, Spain, Colombia and North Africa.

Peyton Anderson
CEO, Affinergy, Inc.

The best advice I ever got was on February 7, 1998 at a local conference on entrepreneurship. I have had the notes taped to my office wall ever since then. A wonderful person and entrepreneur, Robbie Hardy, shared her top 10 keys to being a successful entrepreneur:

1. Practice listening

2. Surround yourself with smart people

3. Spend investors' money wisely

4. Articulate and share a vision

5. Trust and respect your partners

6. Have unlimited stamina and passion

7. Don't take yourself too seriously

8. Focus, focus, focus

9. Develop a sense of humor

10. Leverage your ego, don't bronze it.

About Peyton Anderson

Peyton is a successful entrepreneur who co-founded SciQuest, Inc. in 1995 as its founding CEO. SciQuest raised over $175 million in capital, including a successful Initial Public Offering in 1999. His responsibilities included raising capital, recruiting the management team, doing strategic partner deals, and orchestrating 8 acquisitions.

Peyton joined Affinergy as CEO in September 2003. Since that time, Affinergy has secured $5m in investor funding, recruited a Board of Directors, and negotiated partnership agreements. Affinergy is now positioned as a platform technology in the rapidly growing market for combination products.

Peyton currently serves on the Board of Directors of the North Carolina Biotechnology Center and he has served on the executive committee of the Board of Directors for the Council for Entrepreneurial Development. He is a frequent speaker at entrepreneurial conferences and MBA classes. Peyton graduated Phi Beta Kappa from the U. of Richmond in 1989 and earned his MBA from UNC's Kenan Flagler Business School in 1995.

About the Author

Paul B. Thornton is a speaker, author, consultant, and associate professor of business administration at Springfield Technical Community College in Springfield, Massachusetts. In addition, he is an associate professor at large for The Thierry Graduate School of Leadership located in Brussels, Belgium. Through seminars and individual coaching he helps executives, managers, and organizations reach their potential.

Paul has designed and conducted management/leadership programs for many companies including: AmberWave Systems, Mercy Health Systems, Palmer Foundry, UMASS Medical School, Management Development International, Kuwait Oil Corporation, and United Technologies Corporation. Since 1980 he has trained over 10,000 supervisors and managers to be more effective leaders.

Paul has designed and conducted management/leadership programs for many companies. He is the author of numerous articles and 13 books on management and leadership. His latest books include:

- *Leadership-Best Advice I Ever Got*—available at amazon.com
- *The Big Three Management Styles*—available at *Multi-Media Publications (www.mmpubs.com)*
- *Big Leadership Ideas—Foremost Press*—available at amazon.com and www.foremostpress.com

Did you like this book?

If you enjoyed this book, you will find more interesting books at

www.MMPubs.com

Please take the time to let us know how you liked this book. Even short reviews of 2-3 sentences can be helpful and may be used in our marketing materials. If you take the time to post a review for this book on Amazon.com, let us know when the review is posted and you will receive a free audiobook or ebook from our catalog. Simply email the link to the review once it is live on Amazon.com, with your name, and your mailing address—send the email to orders@mmpubs. com with the subject line "Book Review Posted on Amazon."

If you have questions about this book, our customer loyalty program, or our review rewards program, please contact us at info@mmpubs.com.

Multi-Media
P u b l i c a t i o n s Inc.

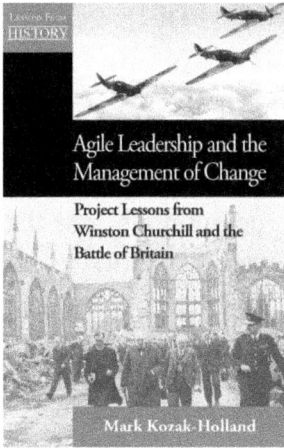

Agile Leadership and the Management of Change

A poll conducted in Britain asked who people thought was the most influential person in all of Britain's history. The winner: Winston Churchill. What set Churchill above the others was his leadership qualities: his ability to create and share a powerful vision, his ability to motivate the population in the face of tremendous fear, and his ability to get others to rally behind him and quickly turn his visions into reality. By any measure, Winston Churchill was a powerful leader.

What many don't know, however, was how Churchill used his leadership skills to restructure the British military, government, and even the British manufacturing sector to support his efforts to rearm the country and get ready for an imminent enemy invasion in early 1940. A lot can be learned about how he managed this enormous change effort. Fortunately, documents and other evidence exists that explains how he did it. Join author Mark Kozak-Holland as he explores how Churchill acted as the head project manager of a massive change project that affected the daily lives of millions of people. Learn about Churchill's change management and agile management techniques and how they can be applied to today's projects.

ISBN: 9781554890354 (paperback)

Also available in ebook formats.
http://www.mmpubs.com/

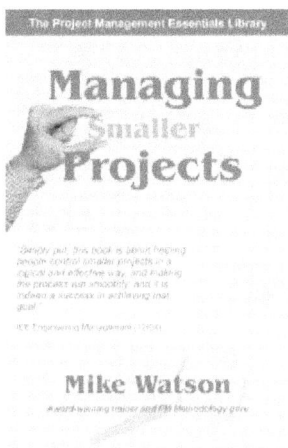

Managing Smaller Projects: A Practical Approach

So called "small projects" can have potentially alarming consequences if they go wrong, but their control is often left to chance. The solution is to adapt tried and tested project management techniques.

This book provides a low overhead, highly practical way of looking after small projects. It covers all the essential skills: from project start-up, to managing risk, quality and change, through to controlling the project with a simple control system. It cuts through the jargon of project management and provides a framework that is as useful to those lacking formal training, as it is to those who are skilled project managers and want to control smaller projects without the burden of bureaucracy.

Read this best-selling book from the U.K., now making its North American debut. *IEE Engineering Management* praises the book, noting that "Simply put, this book is about helping people control smaller projects in a logical and effective way, and making the process run smoothly, and is indeed a success in achieving that goal."

Available in print format.
Order from your favourite bookseller or directly from the publisher at **www.mmpubs.com/msp**

www.ingramcontent.com/pod-product-compliance
Lightning Source LLC
LaVergne TN
LVHW021544080426
835509LV00019B/2827